FIRST 50 CHORDS

YOU SHOULD PLAY ON GUITAR

by Doug Boduch

ISBN 978-1-5400-6233-8

World headquarters, contact:
Hal Leonard
7777 West Bluemound Road
Milwaukee, WI 53213
Email: info@halleonard.com

In Europe, contact:
Hal Leonard Europe Limited
1 Red Place
London, W1K 6PL
Email: info@halleonardeurope.com

In Australia, contact:
Hal Leonard Australia Pty. Ltd.
4 Lentara Court
Cheltenham, Victoria, 3192 Australia
Email: info@halleonard.com.au

CONTENTS

INTRODUCTION

Welcome to the *First 50 Chords You Should Play on Guitar*. Throughout this book, you will find some of the most popular and most often used guitar chords. Included will be a grid showing you how to play the chord as well as a photo. Each chord will have a quick tip with some information about how to play the chord effectively. We've also included a short popular song excerpt that uses each chord. Many of the song excerpts will also feature additional chords taught in the book. Occasionally, there will be a chord that isn't featured in the book, but we'll provide a chord diagram so you can still learn the chord.

When first learning a new chord, the most difficult thing may be getting all notes to ring clearly. Many times, a finger on a fret may accidentally mute another string. Make sure your left-hand fingers are standing as straight up as possible to avoid muting strings below them, focusing on using your fingertips. Play each note of the chord individually to be sure all notes ring. Try to get as close to the fret as possible without touching it. After your chord sounds clear, the next hurdle will be to change chords quickly. This won't happen overnight, so don't get discouraged! Keep working on transitioning the chords and trying to move the fingers as a unit instead of placing them down individually. With enough practice, you'll soon be changing chords effortlessly with no gaps in between.

We've organized the chords into several different categories:

Open Major Chords: These will be the "happy" sounding chords. Major chords are made up of three notes called a *triad*, and on the guitar we repeat some of those notes with octaves to make the chord sound big. The term "open" refers to the use of open strings and playing within the first few frets.

Open Minor Chords: These will be the "sad" sounding chords. They are also made up of three notes, but in this case, one of the notes is lowered in comparison to a major chord, and this creates the minor interval.

Open Dominant Seventh Chords: These chords will have a bit of a "tense" sound to them, leaving the listener wanting a resolution. They are very popular in jazz and blues music.

Open Minor Seventh Chords: These chords will have a bit more color to them than just a minor chord, yet they still have a melancholy sound.

Open Major Seventh Chords: These chords will have a very "sweet" sound to them.

Open Added-Color Chords: These chords will stray from the pure triad format and will have a more "colorful" sound. Often times, you can use them in place of a major chord to get a richer sound.

Power Chords: These chords can be found in almost any rock song. Technically, they're not really "chords," but *dyads*, as they have only two notes. But they are a staple in guitar playing. They sound great with distortion and are easy to move around the neck.

Barre Chords: These will be the toughest chords in the book to play, but they're also some of the most versatile. You'll need to use your first finger to hold down several strings. Keep it as flat as possible and don't squeeze too hard, but rather try to use your strength from the bigger pulling muscles of the shoulder and arm.

Triads: These chords will look similar to ones that you played in the open position. Just like barre chords, we can make a brand new chord by simply moving them up the neck. They're very popular with reggae, funk, and R&B.

Slash Chords: These are some of the most confusing chords for students. They're not difficult to play, but many students don't understand what they are. At first glance, many students think it's an option as to what chord to play. Sorry, that's not the case! Simply put, the first letter is the actual sounding chord, and the second letter is the lowest note of the chord. Most times, chords will be rooted on their note name. For example, a G chord's lowest note will be a G. But with slash chords, we have a different lowest note that is not the root of the chord.

Altered Chords: Altered chords are the most complex of any in this book. Without getting into theory, they are made up of a triad plus some other notes that give them a very complex sound.

There are a lot more than just 50 chords to learn on guitar, but this will give you a great start!

OPEN MAJOR CHORDS
G

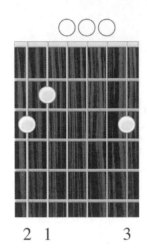

2 1   3

The open G chord is one of the most popular chords on the guitar, making use of all six strings. Although the common way to finger it is with the first, second, and third fingers, the use of the second, third, and fourth fingers instead will make transitioning to the often-used C chord much easier. Another voicing of the G chord, which adds the third fret D on the second string, will make the common transition from a Cadd9 chord a simple matter of moving only two fingers.

"Knockin' on Heaven's Door"

Chorus

Knock, knock, knock - in' on heav - en's door.

Knock, knock, knock - in' on heav - en's door.

Words and Music by Bob Dylan
Copyright © 1973, 1976 Ram's Horn Music
International Copyright Secured   All Rights Reserved
Used by Permission

Alternate Fingerings:

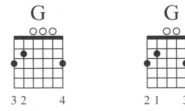

G   G

3 2   4   2 1 3 4

OPEN MAJOR CHORDS
C

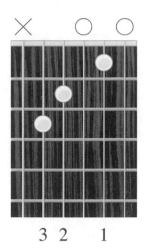

The open C chord is another very popular chord on the guitar. Strum from the fifth string down, making sure not to hit the sixth string. Also, take care to use the tip of your first finger so it doesn't block the open first string. When first practicing, play each note of the chord individually to make sure they all ring clearly. The alternate voicing adds a higher-pitched flavor to the chord.

"Patience"

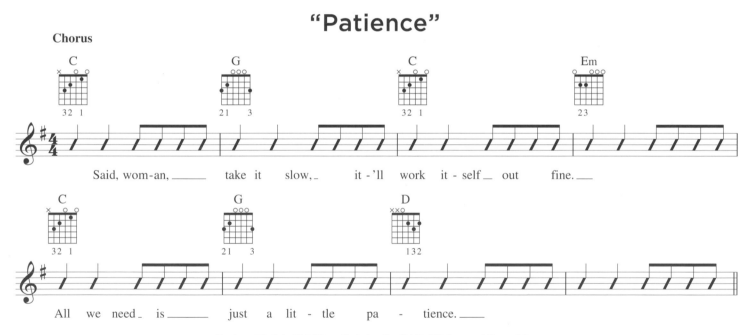

Chorus

C   G   C   Em

Said, wom-an, _____ take it slow,_ it -'ll work it - self _ out fine. _____

C   G   D

All we need _ is _____ just a lit - tle pa - tience. _____

Alternate Voicing:

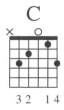

C

3 2 1 4

OPEN MAJOR CHORDS
D

1 3 2

The open D chord uses only the last four strings. Be careful to not strum the fifth or sixth strings, and be sure to use the tip of the ring finger so it doesn't mute the first string.

"Bad Moon Rising"

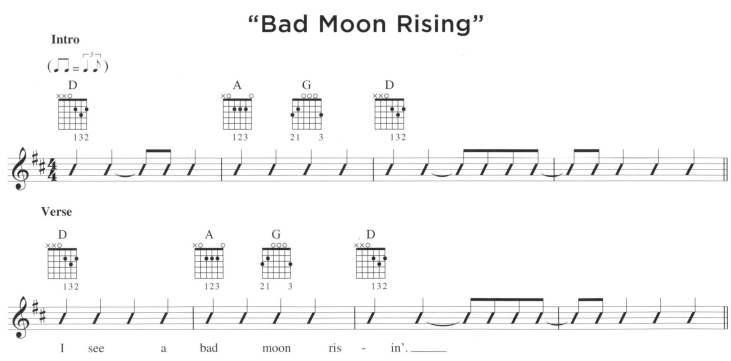

I see a bad moon ris - in'. _____

Words and Music by John Fogerty
Copyright © 1969 Jondora Music c/o Concord Music Publishing
Copyright Renewed
International Copyright Secured   All Rights Reserved

OPEN MAJOR CHORDS
A

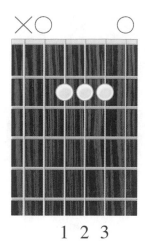

The A chord can be one of the trickier open chords to play. You have to try to squeeze three fingers all on one fret. Some players have more luck with the alternate fingering that tucks the first finger in between the second and third. Another option is to use a technique called a *barre* where you use one flattened finger to fret three strings. Unless you're blessed with a very flexible finger, don't worry about getting that open first string to ring when using the barre. When playing the song excerpt below, try playing only the lowest note of the chord on the first and third beats of each measure, and then strum the full chord on beats two and four.

"Take Me Home, Country Roads"

Alternate Fingerings:

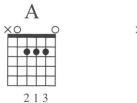

OPEN MAJOR CHORDS

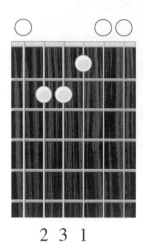

2 3 1

The open E chord uses all six strings with the sixth, second, and first all ringing open. The alternate fingering shown below is useful when moving to other barre chords, which you'll learn later in the book.

"Melissa"

Alternate Fingering:

E

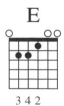

3 4 2

OPEN MAJOR CHORDS
F

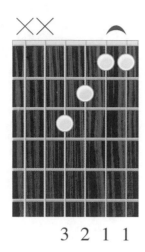

3 2 1 1

The F chord is the most difficult open position chord to play. It requires the use of a small barre with the first finger covering both the first and second strings. Meanwhile, you still need to be on the tips of your second and third fingers. It uses only the last four strings, so be sure not to strum the fifth or sixth strings. Don't get too discouraged if you have trouble with this chord; it can take a while to get comfortable enough to play it.

"Let It Be"

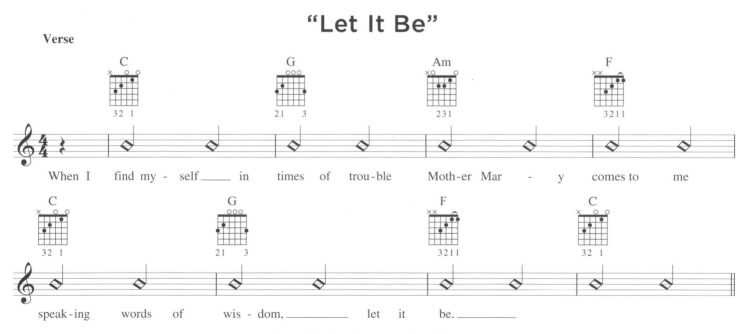

OPEN MINOR CHORDS
Am

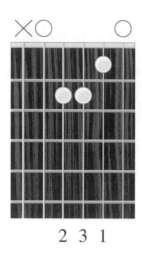

2 3 1

The Am (pronounced "A minor") chord uses five strings and is very similar to the C chord that you learned previously in the book. Play the C chord first, and then take your ring finger off the fifth string, putting it on the second fret of the third string. Since the C chord is often used in succession with the Am, it's a good idea to practice this transition. This will also help with the skill of keeping some fingers down while moving others. Of course, when you need to play an Am chord, don't play the C chord first, but rather use it as a visual reference to help you remember the Am. Also, notice that the difference between the A and the Am is only one fret. Note that the alternate fingering for the Am will be helpful when using some barre chords learned later in the book.

"Riptide"

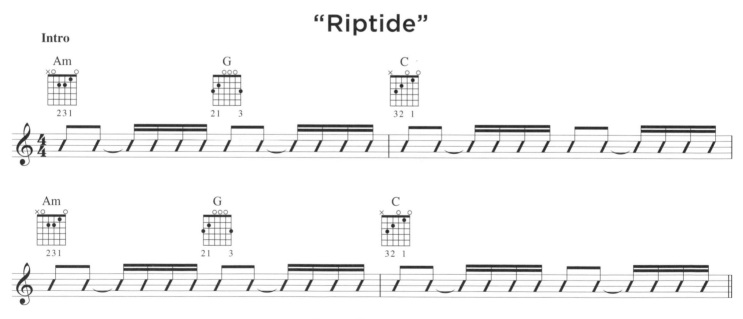

Words and Music by Vance Joy
© 2013 WC MUSIC CORP. and VANCE JOY ASCAP PUB DESIGNEE
All Rights Administered by WC MUSIC CORP.
All Rights Reserved   Used by Permission

Alternate Fingering:

Am

3 4 2

OPEN MINOR CHORDS
Em

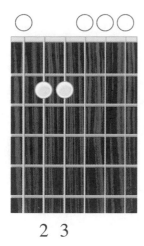

The Em chord is one of the most used and easiest chords to play on the guitar. It uses all six strings and has only two fretted notes with four open strings being played. Again, notice that the Em chord is only one note different than the E chord. Depending on which chord is after Em in a song, you might want to use a different fingering. It's always a good idea to use common fingers between two chords. In other words, if you can finger a chord so that you're using one or more of the same fingers and frets for the next chord, keep those fingers planted, and it will make the transition easier. Don't be scared by the name of the second chord in the song excerpt, D§/F♯. It's really just an easy chord with a complicated name!

"A Horse With No Name"

Intro

Em   D§/F♯   Em   D§/F♯

Alternate Fingerings:

Em   Em

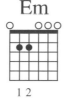

1 2   3 4

OPEN MINOR CHORDS
Dm

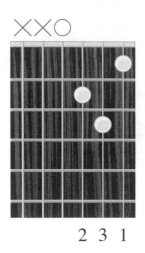

XXO

2 3 1

Dm is perhaps the saddest sounding of all the minor chords. It is again only one note different than its major relative, D. Be sure to play only the highest four strings.

"Ain't No Sunshine"

Verse

Am
231

Em
23

Ain't no sun - shine when she's gone, _____ and she's al - ways gone too

Dm
231

Am
231

Em
23

G
21 3

long an - y - time _____ she goes a - way._____

Words and Music by Bill Withers
Copyright © 1971 INTERIOR MUSIC CORP.
Copyright Renewed
All Rights Controlled and Administered by SONGS OF UNIVERSAL, INC.
All Rights Reserved   Used by Permission

OPEN DOMINANT SEVENTH CHORDS
E7

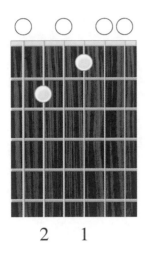

To play an E7 chord, fret an E and simply lift off your third finger, allowing the fourth string to ring open. Visualize this move when memorizing the fingering. It always helps to reference a new chord with one that you already know. Check out the alternate voicing as well, where you take an E chord and just add the pinky to the second string, third fret. It's a more difficult chord to play, but it offers a slightly different sounding chord.

"Wild World"

Words and Music by Cat Stevens
Copyright © 1970 Salafa Limited
Copyright Renewed
All Rights Administered by BMG Rights Management (US) LLC
All Rights Reserved   Used by Permission

Alternate Voicing:

E7

2 3 1 4

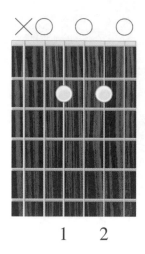

The A7 chord uses five strings, three of which are open. View it as an A chord with an open third string. Make sure you play with your fingertips so the open strings ring clearly. Again, the alternate fingerings will be useful depending on which chord follows the A7. The alternate voicings, although more difficult to play, add a different flavor to the sound.

"Twist and Shout"

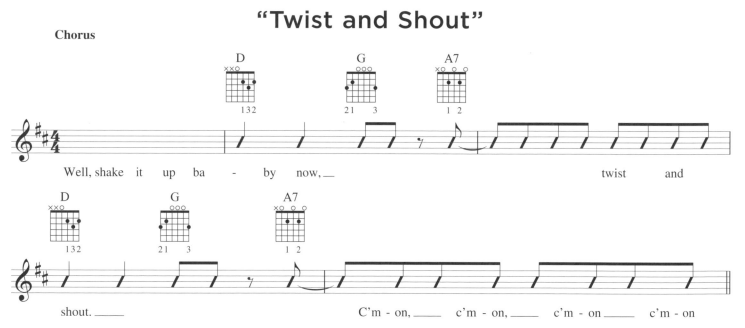

Chorus

Well, shake it up ba - by now, ___ twist and

shout. ___ C'm - on, ___ c'm - on, ___ c'm - on ___ c'm - on

Words and Music by Bert Russell and Phil Medley
Copyright © 1964 Sony/ATV Music Publishing LLC and Sloopy II Music
Copyright Renewed
All Rights on behalf of Sony/ATV Music Publishing LLC Administered by Sony/ATV Music Publishing LLC, 424 Church Street, Suite 1200, Nashville, TN 37219
All Rights on behalf of Sloopy II Music Administered by Wren Music Co., A Division of MPL Music Publishing, Inc.
International Copyright Secured   All Rights Reserved

Alternate Fingerings and Voicings:

OPEN DOMINANT SEVENTH CHORDS
C7

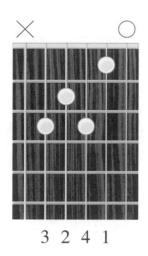

3 2 4 1

To play the C7 chord, simply play a C chord and add the pinky on the third string, third fret. Again, make sure to use your fingertips when fretting to get the open first string to ring clearly.

"Mustang Sally"

Verse

C7
3241

Mus - tang Sal - ly,   huh,   huh,

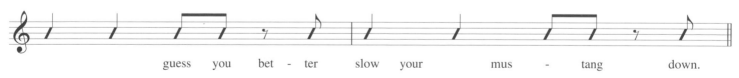

guess you bet - ter slow your mus - tang down.

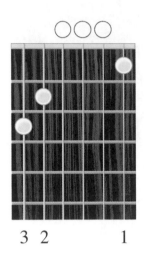

3 2   1

The G7 chord requires the stretch of the fingers, spanning all six strings. Note that it is different from the G chord by only one note. Such is the case with the minor and seventh chords that we've learned so far. Visualization is very important in learning and memorizing chords, so always use what you know as a reference.

"Hey, Good Lookin'"

Hey, hey, _____ good _ look-in' what - cha got cook-in'?

How's a-bout cook - in' __ some-thin' up _____ with me? _____

B7

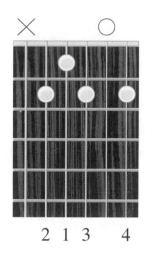

The B7 chord can be a difficult one to finger, as you'll need to line up three fingers all on the second fret. It is often followed or preceded by an E chord, so it's a good idea to work on that transition.

"Summertime Blues"

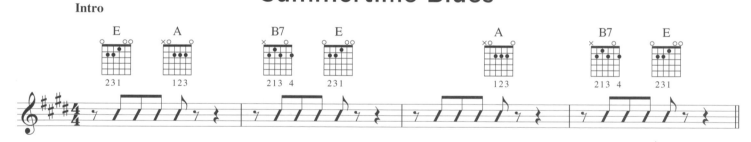

OPEN DOMINANT SEVENTH CHORDS
D7

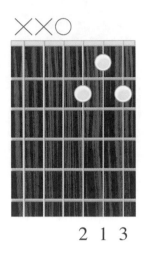

2 1 3

Note that the D7 chord is like a mirror image of the D. We simply move the third fret on the second string to the first fret. It requires a completely different fingering, but seeing it this way can help you memorize it.

"Brown Eyed Girl"

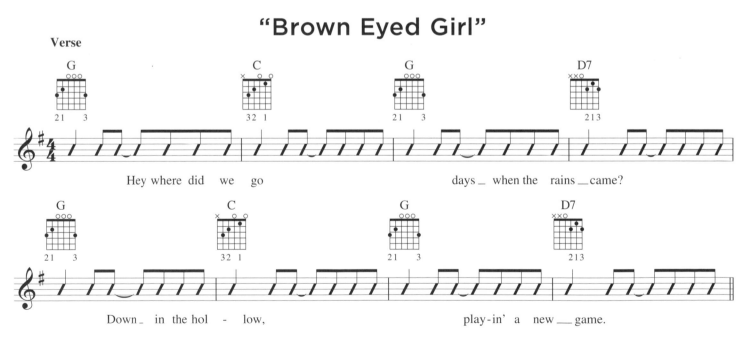

OPEN MINOR SEVENTH CHORDS
Em7

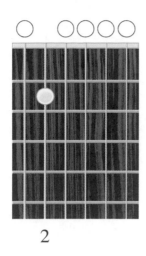

2

Em7 is by far the easiest chord in the book. It only uses one finger! Check out the alternate voicings to add even more color to this chord. The second alternate voicing works great when preceded by a four-finger G chord, as you only need to remove your second finger.

"I Need You"

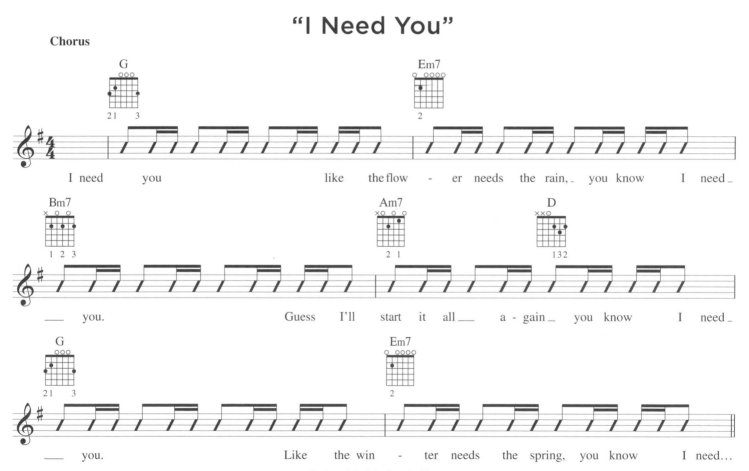

Chorus

G   Em7

I need you   like the flow - er needs the rain,_ you know I need _

Bm7   Am7   D

____ you.   Guess I'll start it all ___ a - gain_ you know I need _

G   Em7

____ you.   Like the win - ter needs the spring, you know I need...

Alternate Fingerings and Voicings:

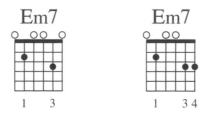

Em7   Em7

1   3   1   3 4

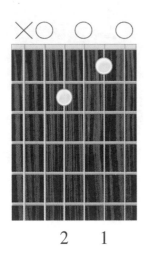

An easy way to think of Am7 is as a C chord without the third finger. Use those fingertips so the open notes can ring! The alternate voicing works well when coming from a four-finger C chord.

"100 Years"

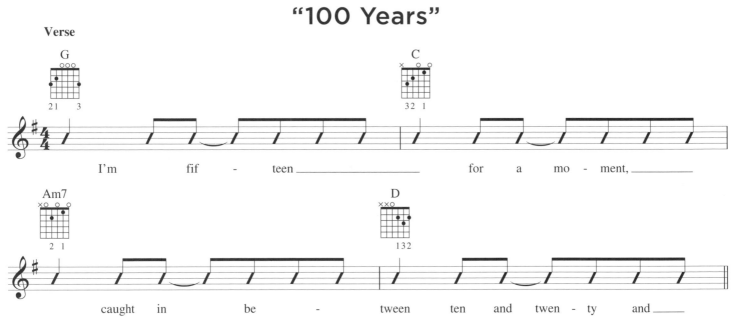

I'm fif - teen _____ for a mo - ment, _____

caught in be - tween ten and twen - ty and _____

Alternate Voicing:

Am7

2 1 4

OPEN MINOR SEVENTH CHORDS
Dm7

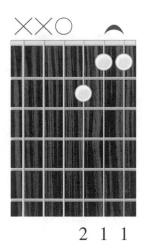

XXO

2 1 1

As you may have noticed, the minor seventh chords we've learned have been only one note different than their respective minor chord. Again, this is the case with Dm7 having one note different than Dm. You can also view it as an F chord but without the third finger.

"Just the Way You Are"

Chorus

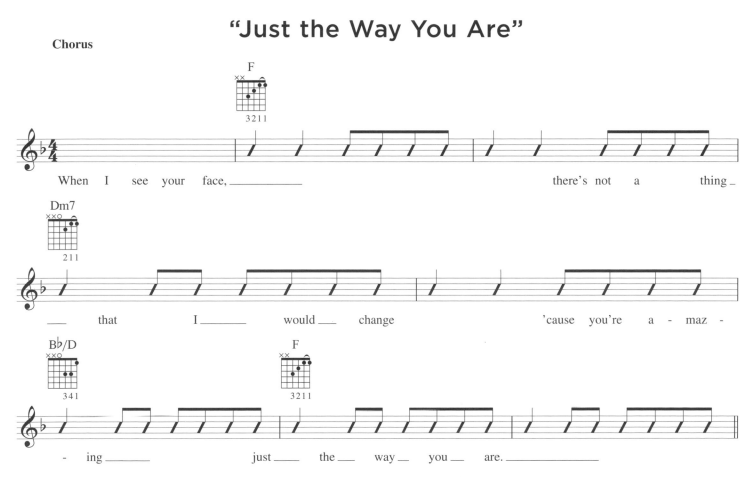

When I see your face, _____ there's not a thing _

___ that I ___ would ___ change 'cause you're a - maz -

- ing _____ just ___ the ___ way ___ you ___ are. _____

OPEN MAJOR SEVENTH CHORDS
Amaj7

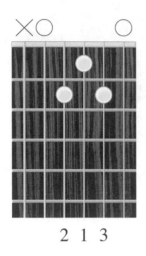

2 1 3

By simply changing one note from the A major chord, we get the sweet sound of the Amaj7. It's not a chord you can use in place of an A, but its unique sound has found its way into many songs.

"Time"

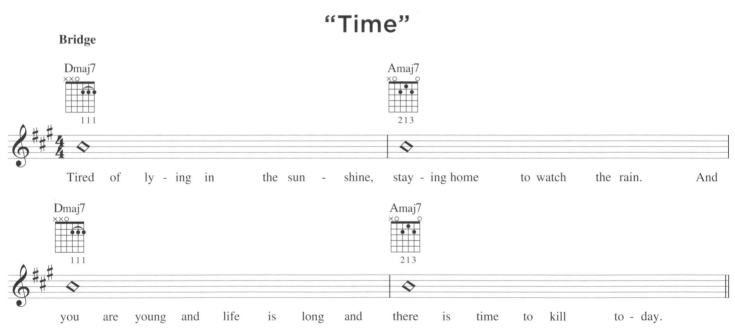

Bridge

Dmaj7
111

Amaj7
213

Tired of ly - ing in the sun - shine, stay - ing home to watch the rain. And

Dmaj7
111

Amaj7
213

you are young and life is long and there is time to kill to - day.

OPEN MAJOR SEVENTH CHORDS
Fmaj7

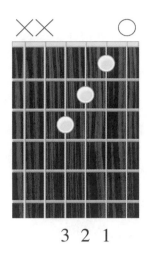

3 2 1

The Fmaj7 chord takes out the tricky element of having to barre two strings, as in the F chord. Since the open first string is what sets this chord apart, make sure it's ringing clearly.

"One"

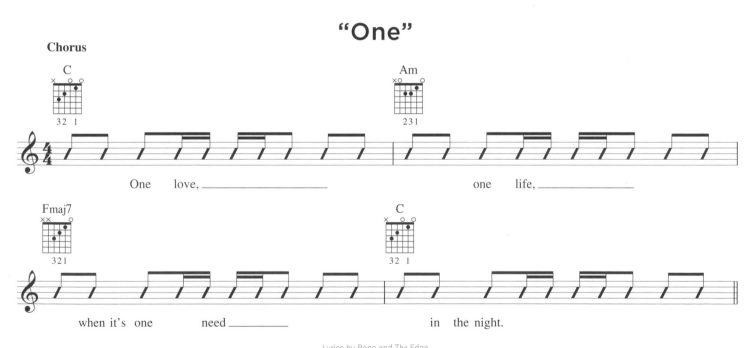

Chorus

C

Am

One love, _____ one life, _____

Fmaj7

C

when it's one need _____ in the night.

Lyrics by Bono and The Edge
Music by U2

OPEN MAJOR SEVENTH CHORDS
Cmaj7

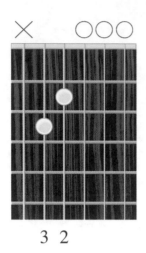

3 2

To play Cmaj7, simply lift off the first finger of a C chord. With the top three strings ringing open, the chord has a very ethereal, celestial sound. For the song excerpt, try strumming the full chord on the downbeat and playing the bass note on the upbeats, creating the pattern "full strum–bass note–full strum–bass note," etc. Use all downstrokes for this pattern.

"Imagine"

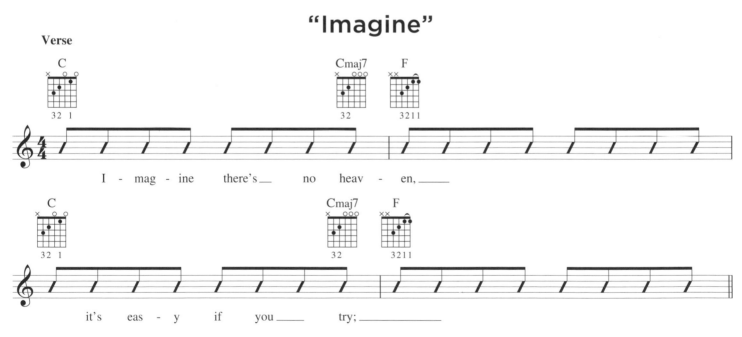

Verse

C   Cmaj7   F

I - mag - ine   there's___   no   heav - en, _____

C   Cmaj7   F

it's   eas - y   if   you _____   try; _____

Words and Music by John Lennon
© 1971 (Renewed) LENONO MUSIC
All Rights Administered by DOWNTOWN DMP SONGS/DOWNTOWN MUSIC PUBLISHING LLC
All Rights Reserved   Used by Permission

OPEN MAJOR SEVENTH CHORDS
Gmaj7

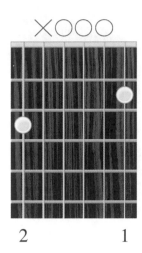

At first glance, Gmaj7 would appear to be an easy chord, as it uses only two fingers. The trick, however, is that we don't want the fifth string to sound, so we need to mute it with a slightly flattened second finger. It should touch the fifth string just enough to mute it. The alternate voicing adds a bit more flavor to the top end of the chord. For the song excerpt, in addition to strumming, you can also try "arpeggiating" or playing the notes of the chord separately. Start with the bass note first and then add some higher strings.

"Photographs and Memories"

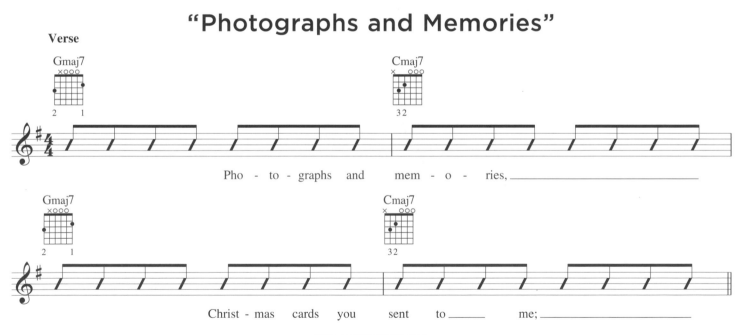

Alternate Voicing:

Gmaj7(no3rd)

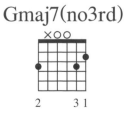

Dmaj7

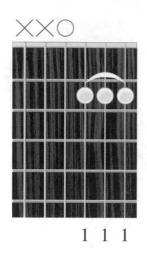

Use the first finger to barre across the highest three strings for the Dmaj7. As it uses only four strings, be careful not to strum the fifth and sixth strings. If the barre gives you trouble, you can use three different fingers to fret the notes. In the end, the barre will be a technique you'll want to master.

"Ventura Highway"

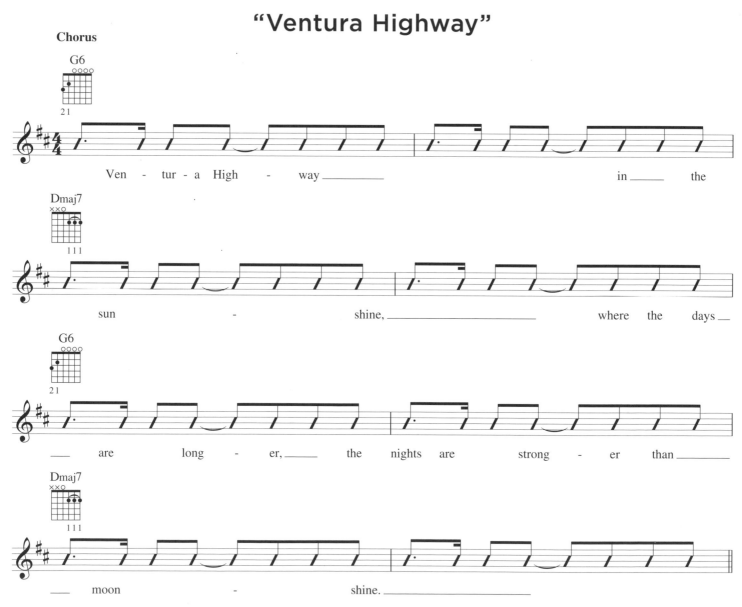

OPEN ADDED-COLOR CHORDS
Cadd9

Without getting into too much theory, the Cadd9 chord has its name because it contains all the notes of a C chord (C–E–G) plus an added ninth degree of the C major scale, D. It can often be used in place of a standard C chord to add a little extra flavor, but know that it is more than just a C chord. It's used a lot when changing from the four-finger G chord that we learned earlier. When changing from the four-finger G chord to the Cadd9, keep the third and fourth fingers planted on the second and first strings, respectively.

"Good Riddance (Time of Your Life)"

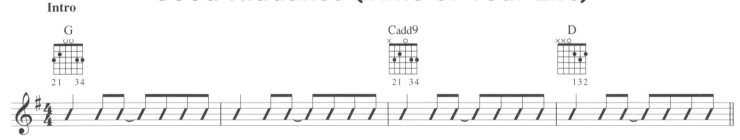

Words by Billie Joe
Music by Green Day
© 1997 WC MUSIC CORP. and GREEN DAZE MUSIC
All Rights Administered by WC MUSIC CORP.
All Rights Reserved   Used by Permission

OPEN ADDED-COLOR CHORDS
Dsus2

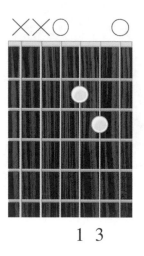

1 3

In a suspended chord, the third is omitted and replaced with either a second or a fourth. In the case of the Dsus2, we omit the F♯ and replace it with an E. It's best to finger it as you would a D chord, since many times a D chord will follow, allowing us to just add the second finger.

"Mary Jane's Last Dance"

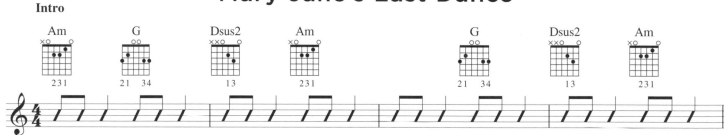

Words and Music by Tom Petty
Copyright © 1993 Gone Gator Music
All Rights Reserved   Used by Permission

OPEN ADDED-COLOR CHORDS
Dsus4

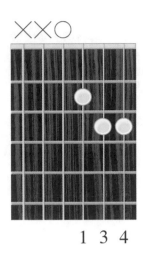

1 3 4

The Dsus4 chord omits the F♯ and replaces it with a G. Note that in our song excerpt, we're moving back and forth between the D and Dsus4, so keep the D fully fingered and just add the pinky to get the Dsus4. That way, to get back to the D, all you need to do is lift up the pinky. Keep an eye out for transitions like this in other songs as well.

"Crazy Little Thing Called Love"

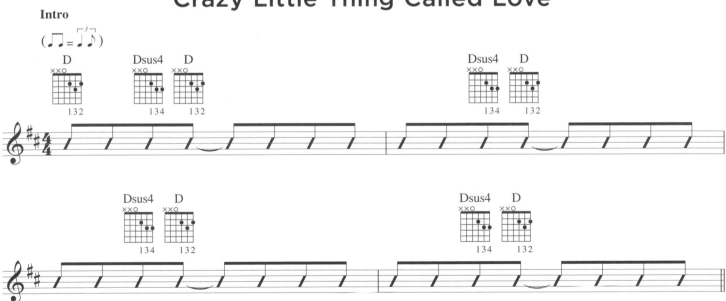

Words and Music by Freddie Mercury
Copyright © 1979 Queen Music Ltd.
All Rights Administered by Sony/ATV Music Publishing LLC, 424 Church Street, Suite 1200, Nashville, TN 37219
International Copyright Secured   All Rights Reserved

OPEN ADDED-COLOR CHORDS
Asus2

1 2

Many times, Asus2 is used in place of an A since it's a bit easier to finger. It's got a great sound for pop music as well. Make sure those two high open strings are ringing!

"Happy Xmas (War Is Over)"

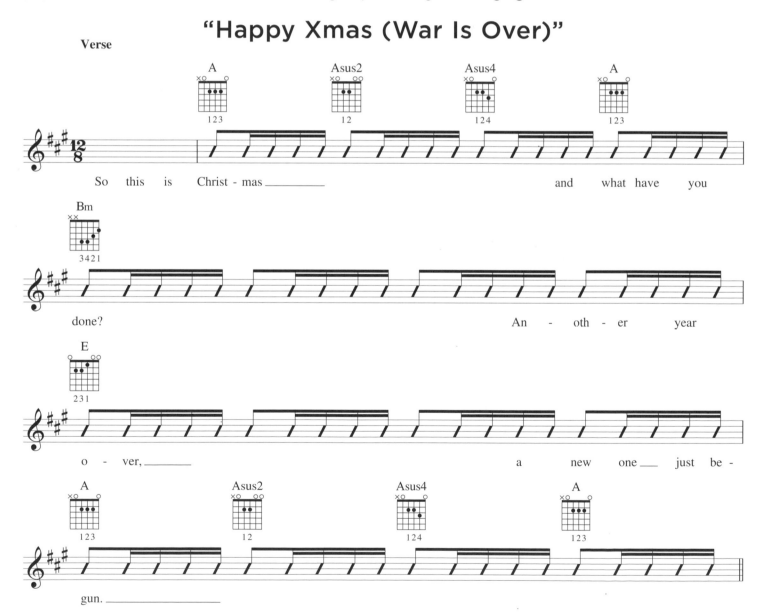

Written by John Lennon and Yoko Ono
© 1971 (Renewed) LENONO MUSIC and ONO MUSIC
Administered in the United States by DOWNTOWN MUSIC PUBLISHING LLC
All Rights Reserved

Asus4

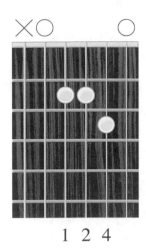

1 2 4

Another staple in pop music is the Asus4 chord. It's got a great "jangly" sound that has found its way into many songs over the years. Using the pinky in this fingering allows an easy transition back to the A, which often occurs in many songs. In our song excerpt below, you'll get to practice all your D and A suspended chords.

"Summer of '69"

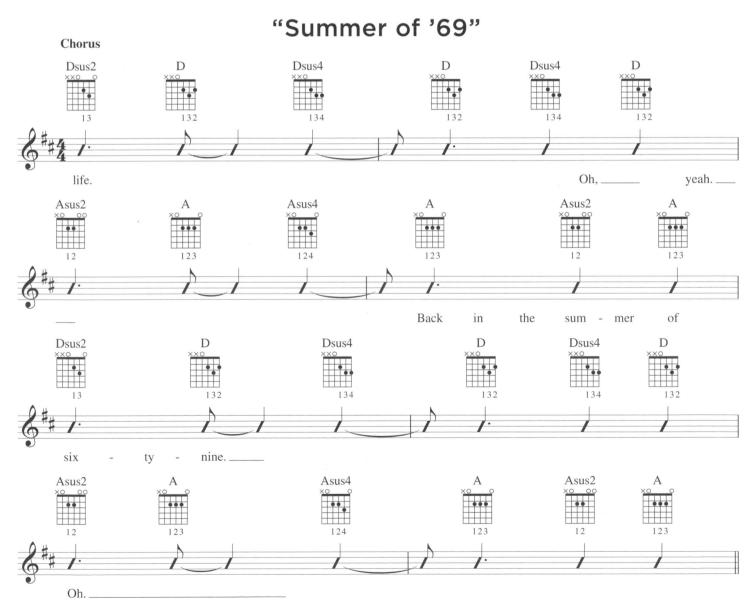

Esus4

2 3 4

The Esus4 chord has a big, bold sound that uses all six strings. Using the pinky for the highest-fretted note allows your first finger to be ready to play the standard E chord, which often follows or precedes the Esus4. Besides being used at the end of the chorus in the song excerpt below, the Esus4 chord is also used exclusively in the intro in an arpeggiated form.

"Behind Blue Eyes"

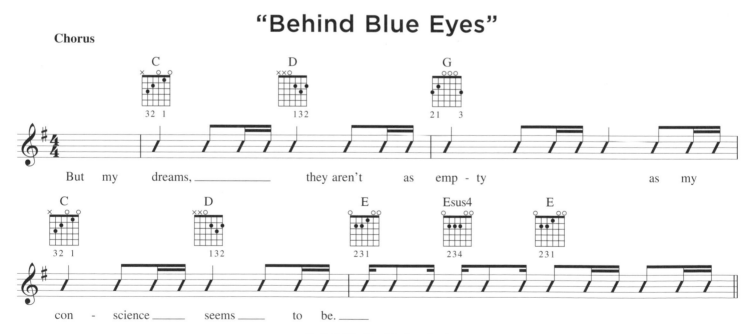

OPEN ADDED-COLOR CHORDS
Gsus4

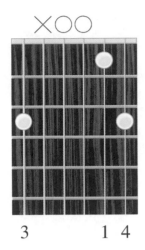

Gsus4 is the trickiest of the suspended chords that we'll learn. It requires a decent stretch between the third and fourth fingers. Also, you'll need to flatten out the third finger a bit so it mutes the fifth string. If you're wondering why we don't play the second fret on the fifth string, it's because that would change the name of the chord to Gadd4. For this suspended chord, we need to omit the third interval (B) and replace it with the fourth (D). Don't worry if all this theory talk confuses you, just focus on playing the chords for now! Notice in the song excerpt below that we're using the alternate fingering for the G chord with the second, third, and fourth fingers. This will make the change to the Gsus4 a little easier.

"You've Got a Friend"

Verse

Am7   D7   G   Gsus4   G   Gsus4

noth-ing, _____ whoa, noth-ing is go - ing _ right, _

POWER CHORDS
A5

1

Being our first example of a power chord, the A5 is one of the easier chords you'll learn—just two notes! You'll find it used a lot in rock songs as well as blues and pop music. It's important to strum only the two notes and not hit any other strings. Work on playing downstrokes first, and then try to add more complicated alternate strum patterns. The alternate voicing simply adds an octave of the root, which makes for a bigger sounding chord. A small first-finger barre will be the best option to finger this alternate voicing.

"Won't Get Fooled Again"

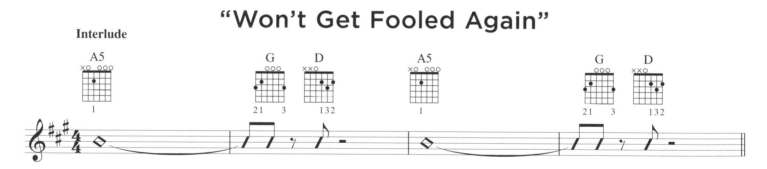

Alternate Voicing:

A5

1 1

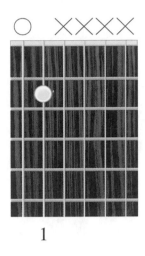

The E5 power chord is just like the A5, but on a different set of strings. All of the same tips apply. Also, practice making the transition from the A5 to the E5. It's easy in the left hand, but your right hand will need to strum the appropriate strings. The following example uses the alternate voicing shown at the bottom of the page in addition to other similar voicings of power chords.

"Back in Black"

Alternate Voicing:

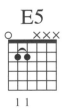

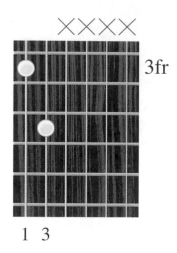

G5 is the first movable chord shape that you'll learn. For example, if you need a G♯5, simply move it up one fret. The lowest note of the chord is the root, and in this case, is on the sixth string. The same principle holds true for the alternate voicings and fingerings.

"More Than a Feeling"

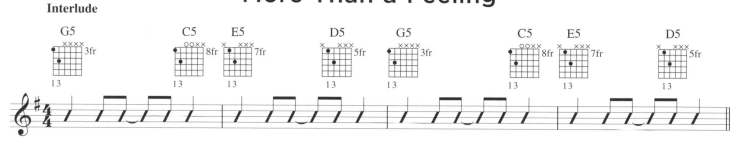

Alternate Fingerings and Voicings:

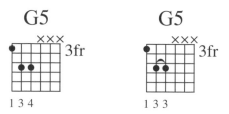

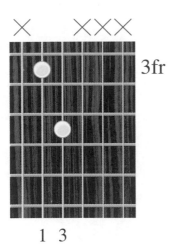

C5 follows the same guidelines as the G5 chord, except that the C5 is rooted on the fifth string. Take care not to hit the low sixth string when playing. To help with that, try touching with just the tip of your index finger to the sixth string. Do this by fretting the fifth string and extend just the tip of your finger a bit so that it touches the sixth string. This will help keep that string quiet if you accidentally hit it. It's also a great safety measure in case you want to do some big rock star strums! If you noticed, we played a different C5 on the last song excerpt. They are the same chord, and actually the same notes, but played on different strings. There are also two new techniques in this song excerpt—palm muting and muted strums. Palm muting (notated with a "P.M.") involves resting the pad of your right hand against the strings where they meet the bridge, producing a slightly muffled sound. A muted strum, notated with "X" note heads, involves lightly touching the strings with your left hand and strumming, producing a "clicky" percussive sound. To achieve this, just lift up slightly from the chord shape with your left hand fingers, keeping contact with the strings but not fretting.

"When I Come Around"

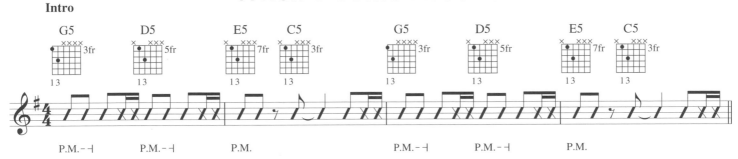

Alternate Fingerings and Voicings:

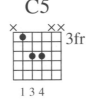

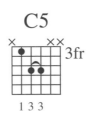

POWER CHORDS
E6

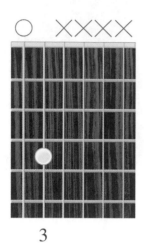

3

In general, E6 isn't a stand-alone chord, but it most often follows an E5. It completes the classic rock and blues shuffle figure, which has defined rock songs from the '60s to the present day. This style is such an integral part of playing guitar that it would be a crime not to include this E6 in a study book of chords.

"Bang a Gong (Get It On)"

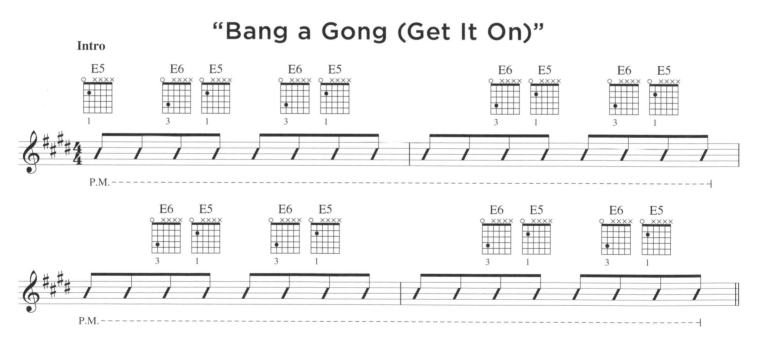

POWER CHORDS
C6

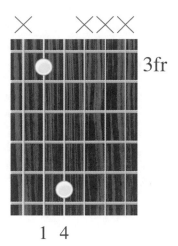

C6 is simply the fretted variation of E6, but rooted on the fifth string. Much like the E6 following the E5, you'll generally play the C6 after a C5, again completing the classic blues rock pattern. But since the C6 is a movable shape, you can now use this pattern all over the neck. Feel free to try this shape after any two-note power chords. It's a big stretch, so you may have some luck working on the chord shape higher up the neck and then moving it down as you develop your stretch. When doing the C5 to C6 move, keep the C5 chord shape planted and just stretch the pinky to fret the C6. Since you'll be changing back and forth on these chords, this will be the most efficient way to play.

"The House Is Rockin'"

Chorus

| C5 | C6 | C5 | | C6 | C5 | | C6 | C5 | | C6 | C5 |

Well, the house ___ is a rock - in', but don't ___ both - er knock - in'. Yeah the

| C6 | C5 | | C6 | C5 | | C6 | C5 | | C6 | C5 |

house ___ is a rock - in', don't ___ both - er knock - in'. Yeah the

BARRE CHORDS
G

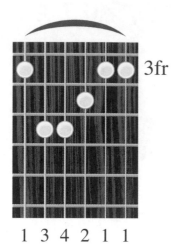

1 3 4 2 1 1

The G barre chord will seem quite difficult at first. Keep your first finger as straight as possible. Before fretting the entire chord, be certain that you can cleanly barre all six strings. Then start adding the other fingers, making sure to keep them curved while using the fingertips. Once you get the hang of this chord, you'll find it to be one of the most versatile that you've learned. It's considered a movable chord, meaning that you can slide the shape around the neck to get different major chords. The note on the sixth string is the root and will determine the name of the chord. Move it up two frets to the fifth fret to get an A chord. Put it on the ninth fret and you have a C♯ chord. With one chord shape, you can play all 12 different major chords! Note that it is nothing more than the open E chord shape moved up while your first finger takes care of covering the open strings. Although the song excerpt has five chords, they are all the same shape. Simply take that G chord and move it around the neck. Try to keep your fingers holding that shape as you move.

"(Sittin' On) The Dock of the Bay"

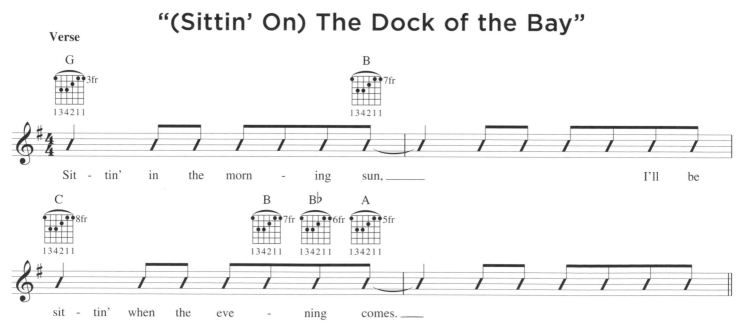

BARRE CHORDS
B

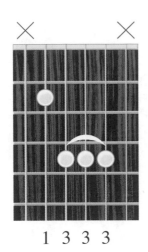

1 3 3 3

The B barre chord is simply the movable version of the open A chord that you previously learned. The most common way to finger this chord is with a third-finger barre. The same principles to barring apply—keep the finger as flat as possible and close to the fret. When played this way, you'll want to barre only the second, third, and fourth strings; angle your finger up a bit so it doesn't fret the first string. Another option is to use the alternate fingering, which employs the first finger to barre across five strings, while the other fingers fret the open A shape. For both fingerings, the root is on the fifth string, and you'll get different major chords by moving it up and down the neck.

"Hold My Hand"

Alternate Fingering:

B

1 2 3 4 1

BARRE CHORDS
Bm

1 3 4 2 1

You'll recognize the barred Bm shape as being the open Am moved up two frets. Again, our first finger will become a "human capo" and take care of those open strings. Also note that it is the same shape as the G barre chord you just learned, but moved down one set of strings. Move this chord around the neck to get all the different minor chords. The root is on the fifth string, so it makes a great exercise for learning the fretboard. If you do the same with the sixth-string-rooted barre chords, then you'll end up learning a good chunk of the neck in no time. Since the sixth string and first string have the same notes, once you learn the fifth string, you'll know three out of the six strings. That's halfway to knowing all the strings! By the way, for the song excerpt below, that four-measure intro gets played for the entire song, so you'll know the whole song by learning these four measures. Play along with the original recording to get some great extended practice on that Bm chord.

"What's Up"

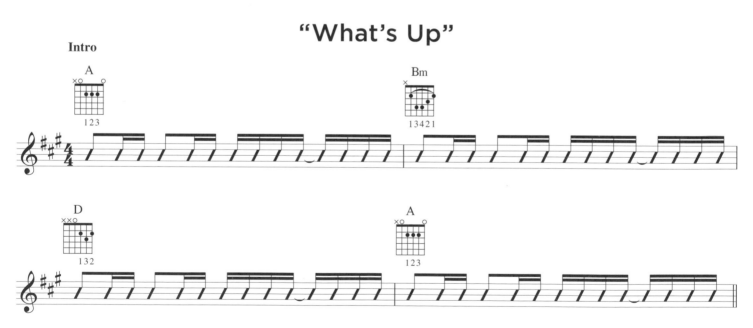

BARRE CHORDS
F♯m

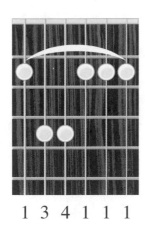

1 3 4 1 1 1

An easy way to remember the F♯m chord is to think of it as the same shape as the G barre chord, but without the second finger. Make sure your first finger is fretting all those strings clearly so you can hear the difference between the major and the minor shape. Also, notice that the last four barre chords you've learned all contain the power chords you learned before. It's very important in learning the guitar to use what you already know to help you understand and remember new chords, scales, etc. If you want to try an easier version of the F♯m, check out the alternate voicing. You'll only have to barre three strings!

"Refugee"

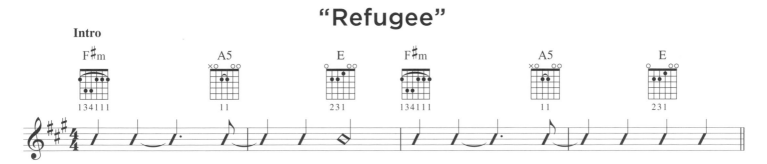

Alternate Voicing:

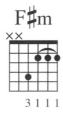

F♯m

3 1 1 1

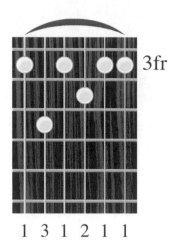

1 3 1 2 1 1

To play the G7 barre, simply play the G barre that you learned and leave off the pinky. It makes for a slightly trickier chord than G, since you'll really need to be on the tip of the third finger to make sure the string below can sound. Again, it's a movable shape with the root on the sixth string, so once you learn the notes of the sixth string, you'll know all 12 dominant seventh chords!

"Hound Dog"

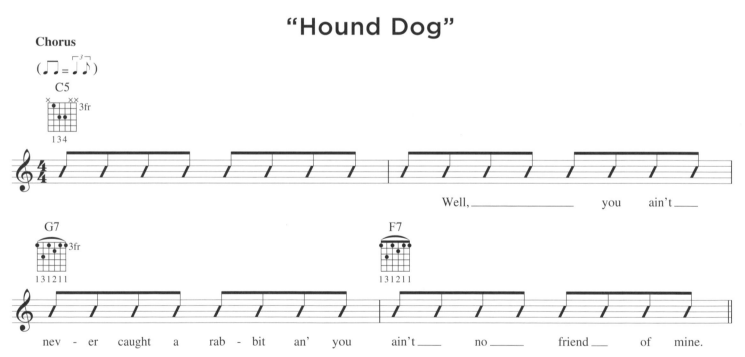

Well,_____ you ain't____

nev - er caught a rab - bit an' you ain't____ no____ friend____ of mine.

Words and Music by Jerry Leiber and Mike Stoller
Copyright © 1953 Sony/ATV Music Publishing LLC
Copyright Renewed
All Rights Administered by Sony/ATV Music Publishing LLC, 424 Church Street, Suite 1200, Nashville, TN 37219
International Copyright Secured All Rights Reserved

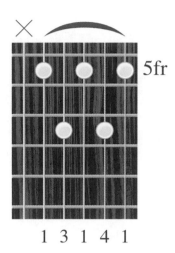

1 3 1 4 1

Notice that the D7 chord shares the same shape as the open A7 that you learned. You'll need to barre across five strings with the first finger, again making sure to use the fingertips of the other fingers when fretting in order to not mute strings below. Notice the muted strum in the song excerpt. Since it falls on the beat right before the chord change, this will give you a little extra time to get to the next chord since the muted strum doesn't need to be fretted. This technique is often used to help make chord transitions smoother. Note that in the song excerpt, the C7 is the same shape as the D7, just moved down two frets. Also, the Am7 is similar to the F#m barre chord shape we learned, just without the pinky and moved up three frets.

"Banana Pancakes"

Verse

G7   D7   Am7   C7

hard-ly   e-ven   no - tice   when   I   try   to   show   you   this

G7   D7   Am7   C7

song;   it's   meant   to   keep ____   you   from   do - ing   what   you're   s'posed __   to.

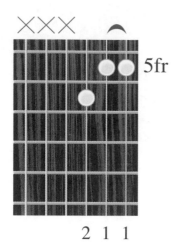

While not usually used as a strum-type chord, this small, three-note A chord will be one of the more versatile chords you'll learn. It is a movable shape just like the barre chords you learned. In fact, if you look at the G barre and move that up two frets to make it an A barre chord, you'll notice that this small A chord is part of that larger chord. So feel free to move this shape around the neck as well, but know that its root is not the lowest note of the chord (in this case it's the highest note). This is referred to as an *inversion*. Even though the chord doesn't have an A root as its lowest note, it still contains the notes necessary to make it an A major triad and still functions the same as any other major chord.

"Me and Julio Down by the Schoolyard"

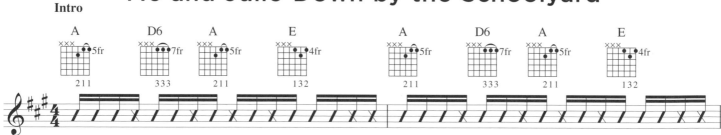

TRIADS
Gm

1 1 1

Another great small-voiced movable chord is the Gm on the third fret. It's played easiest by using the first finger to barre across the top three strings. You can also try using other fingers to barre depending on what other chords come before or after. Again, you'll find the root on the first string. Also notice that this chord is part of the larger sixth-string-rooted minor barre chord shape that you previously learned. Learning chords on the guitar can be overwhelming. It will really help to take what you already know and see the similarities with new chords. Making these connections will help you remember the chords and learn the notes on the fretboard. Watch all the rests in the song excerpt. You can lift your left hand fingers slightly so that the strings stop ringing, but keep them in contact with the strings.

"I Shot the Sheriff"

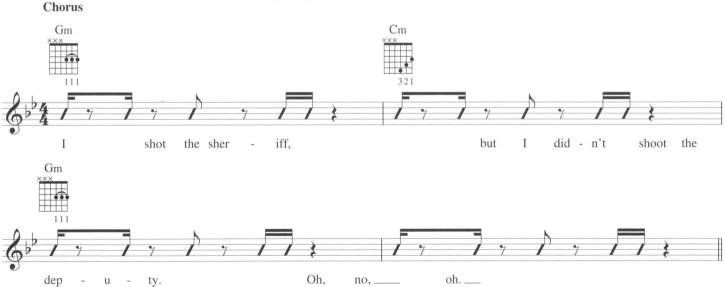

Chorus

Gm — I   shot   the   sher - iff,   Cm — but   I   did - n't   shoot   the

Gm — dep - u - ty.   Oh,   no, ___   oh. ___

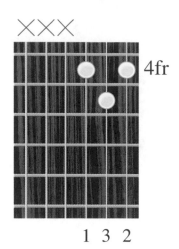

Even though the full open D chord you first learned isn't a common movable shape, if you just use the top three strings, then you have another great small, movable chord shape. In this case, we move that D shape up two frets to make it an E. As you might be able to tell by now, movable chord shapes are very powerful tools on the guitar. You can learn one shape and then instantly have access to 12 different chords just by moving it around the neck. Of course, you'll have to spend some time learning the notes on the fretboard, but that is always time well spent.

"Three Little Birds"

Alternate Fingering:

E

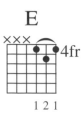

D/F#

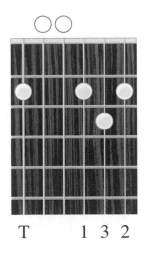

T 1 3 2

Here's another opportunity to take what you already know and build on it. Play the standard open position D major chord, and then wrap your left hand thumb over the neck to fret the sixth string, second fret. What you have now is a D/F♯, pronounced "D over F♯." It's simply a D major chord with an F♯ as the bass or lowest note. You'll see it used a lot as a transition chord between G and Em because it creates a smooth scale descent of the bass notes. If you find fretting with the thumb to be too difficult, check out the alternate fingering which doesn't use the thumb and omits the highest string.

"American Pie"

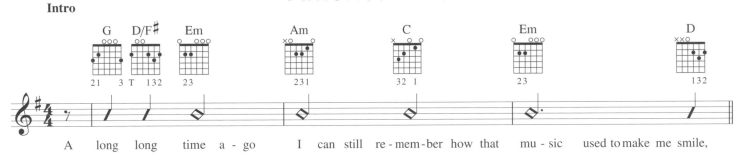

Intro

G   D/F♯   Em   Am   C   Em   D

21   3 T   132   23   231   32 1   23   132

A long long time a-go   I can still re-mem-ber how that   mu-sic   used to make me smile,

Alternate Fingering:

D/F#

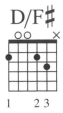

1   2 3

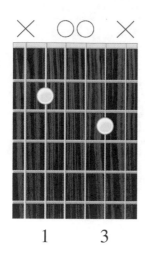

Another popular slash chord is G/B. This time, instead of adding to something you already know, simply take the standard open G chord and simply play only the highest five strings. So it's a G chord, but our lowest note will be the B on the fifth string. You'll find it used frequently as a transition between the C and Am chords, again creating that smooth bass line.

"Landslide"

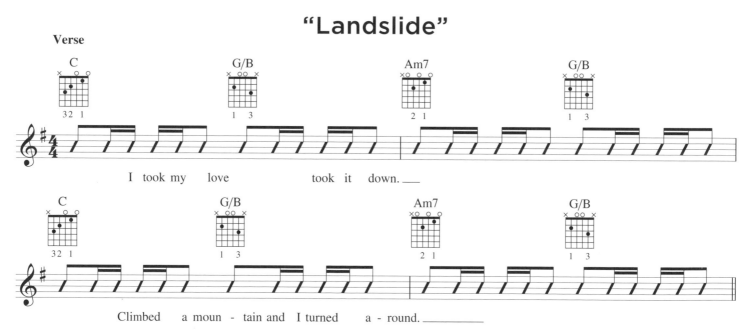

I took my love took it down. ____

Climbed a moun - tain and I turned a - round. _____

Alternate Voicing:

G/B

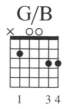

1 3 4

SLASH CHORDS
C/G

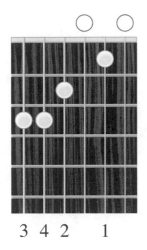

3 4 2   1

To play the C/G chord, you'll need to take the standard C chord and finger it differently. The third finger now frets the lowest G note, with the pinky playing the root C on the fifth string. The C/G chord doesn't sound dramatically different than the C chord, but it does add some richness to the sound.

"Wish You Were Here"

So, so you think you can tell ___ heav-en from hell, ___

blue skies ___ from pain. ___

SLASH CHORDS
G/D

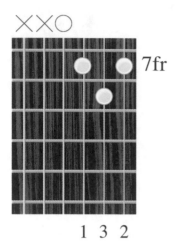

For G/D, we simply take our standard open D chord, move it up five frets, but still play the open D, fourth string. So the movable nature of the small triad shape turns it into a G chord, but we still use the D as the bass note. You can experiment with this shape to create other slash chords. Take the D and move it two frets up while still playing the open fourth string and you'll have an E/D. Move it up another fret and it's F/D. The possibilities are endless! Learning chords doesn't have to be a strict memorization game. Once you have the knowledge of how chords are constructed, you can teach yourself new chords! See if you can make sense of the other slash chords used in the musical example below.

"Give a Little Bit"

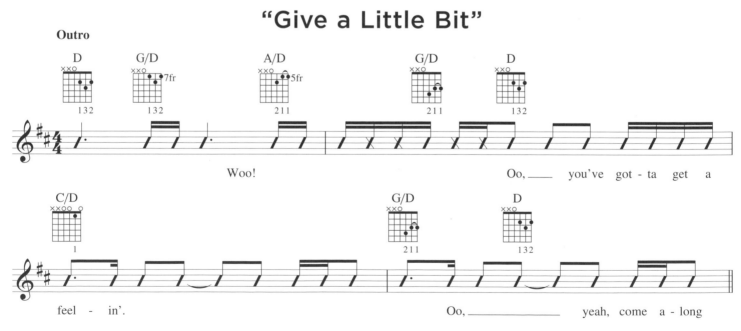

Words and Music by Rick Davies and Roger Hodgson
Copyright © 1977 ALMO MUSIC CORP. and DELICATE MUSIC
Copyright Renewed
All Rights Controlled and Administered by ALMO MUSIC CORP.
All Rights Reserved   Used by Permission

ALTERED CHORDS

D7♯9

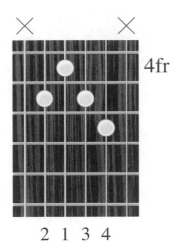

Typically, an altered chord such as this would be found in jazz music. But this chord has found its way into pop, rock, and blues. Since the D7♯9 doesn't have any open strings, it is a movable shape. Move it up two frets to make an E7♯9, which has been commonly referred to as the "Hendrix chord," as he (Jimi Hendrix) used it in one of his popular songs. In simple terms, it's nothing more than a D7 chord with a raised or sharp ninth interval. Again, we take what we know and add to it. While it's not the scope of this book to teach chord theory, I hope this bit of knowledge ignites some interest for you to study the topic. Note that the D7 chord used in the song excerpt is simply the open C7 shape you learned before, but moved up two frets.

"Taxman"

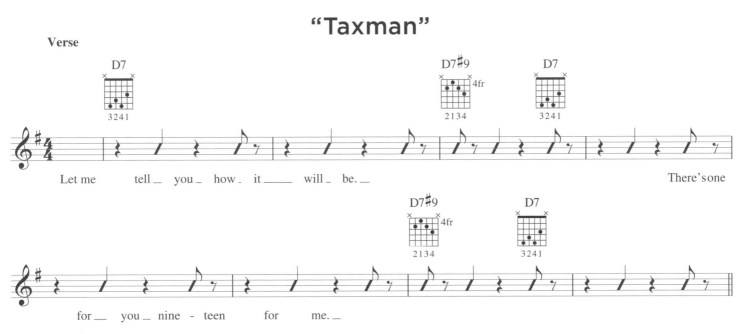

Words and Music by George Harrison
Copyright © 1966 Sony/ATV Music Publishing LLC
Copyright Renewed
All Rights Administered by Sony/ATV Music Publishing LLC, 424 Church Street, Suite 1200, Nashville, TN 37219
International Copyright Secured   All Rights Reserved

FIRST 50

Books in the First 50 series contain easy to intermediate arrangements for must-know songs.
Each arrangement is simple and streamlined, yet still captures the essence of the tune.

First 50 Baroque Pieces
You Should Play on Guitar
Includes selections by Johann Sebastian Bach, Robert de Visée, Ernst Gottlieb Baron, Santiago de Murcia, Antonio Vivaldi, Sylvius Leopold Weiss, and more.
00322567...$14.99

First 50 Bluegrass Solos
You Should Play on Guitar
I Am a Man of Constant Sorrow • Long Journey Home • Molly and Tenbrooks • Old Joe Clark • Rocky Top • Salty Dog Blues • and more.
00298574...$16.99

First 50 Blues Songs
You Should Play on Guitar
All Your Love (I Miss Loving) • Bad to the Bone • Born Under a Bad Sign • Dust My Broom • Hoodoo Man Blues • Little Red Rooster • Love Struck Baby • Pride and Joy • Smoking Gun • Still Got the Blues • The Thrill Is Gone • You Shook Me • and more.
00235790...$17.99

First 50 Blues Turnarounds
You Should Play on Guitar
You'll learn cool turnarounds in the styles of these jazz legends: John Lee Hooker, Robert Johnson, Joe Pass, Jimmy Rogers, Hubert Sumlin, Stevie Ray Vaughan, T-Bone Walker, Muddy Waters, and more.
00277469...$14.99

First 50 Chords
You Should Play on Guitar
American Pie • Back in Black • Brown Eyed Girl • Landslide • Let It Be • Riptide • Summer of '69 • Take Me Home, Country Roads • Won't Get Fooled Again • You've Got a Friend • and more.
00300255 Guitar.....................................$12.99

First 50 Classical Pieces
You Should Play on Guitar
Includes compositions by J.S. Bach, Augustin Barrios, Matteo Carcassi, Domenico Scarlatti, Fernando Sor, Francisco Tárrega, Robert de Visée, Antonio Vivaldi and many more.
00155414...$16.99

First 50 Folk Songs
You Should Play on Guitar
Amazing Grace • Down by the Riverside • Home on the Range • I've Been Working on the Railroad • Kumbaya • Man of Constant Sorrow • Oh! Susanna • This Little Light of Mine • When the Saints Go Marching In • The Yellow Rose of Texas • and more.
00235868...$16.99

First 50 Guitar Duets
You Should Play
Chopsticks • Clocks • Eleanor Rigby • Game of Thrones Theme • Hallelujah • Linus and Lucy (from A Charlie Brown Christmas) • Memory (from Cats) • Over the Rainbow (from The Wizard of Oz) • Star Wars (Main Theme) • What a Wonderful World • You Raise Me Up • and more.
00319706...$14.99

First 50 Jazz Standards
You Should Play on Guitar
All the Things You Are • Body and Soul • Don't Get Around Much Anymore • Fly Me to the Moon (In Other Words) • The Girl from Ipanema (Garota De Ipanema) • I Got Rhythm • Laura • Misty • Night and Day • Satin Summertime • When I Fall in Love • and more.
00198594 Solo Guitar $16.99

First 50 Kids' Songs
You Should Play on Guitar
Do-Re-Mi • Hakuna Matata • Let It Go • My Favorite Things • Puff the Magic Dragon • Take Me Out to the Ball Game • Won't You Be My Neighbor? (It's a Beautiful Day in the Neighborhood) • and more.
00300500 ....$17.99

First 50 Licks
You Should Play on Guitar
Licks presented include the styles of legendary guitarists like Eric Clapton, Buddy Guy, Jimi Hendrix, B.B. King, Randy Rhoads, Carlos Santana, Stevie Ray Vaughan and many more.
00278875 Book/Online Audio..........................$14.99

First 50 Riffs
You Should Play on Guitar
All Right Now • Back in Black • Barracuda • Carry on Wayward Son • Crazy Train • La Grange • Layla • Seven Nation Army • Smoke on the Water • Sunday Bloody Sunday • Sunshine of Your Love • Sweet Home Alabama • Working Man • and more.
00277366...$17.99

First 50 Rock Songs You Should
Play on Electric Guitar
All Along the Watchtower • Beat It • Brown Eyed Girl • Cocaine • Detroit Rock City • Hallelujah • (I Can't Get No) Satisfaction • Oh, Pretty Woman • Pride and Joy • Seven Nation Army • Should I Stay or Should I Go • Smells like Teen Spirit • Smoke on the Water • When I Come Around • You Really Got Me • and more.
00131159 ....$16.99

First 50 Songs by the Beatles You
Should Play on Guitar
All You Need Is Love • Blackbird • Come Together • Eleanor Rigby • Hey Jude • I Want to Hold Your Hand • Let It Be • Ob-La-Di, Ob-La-Da • She Loves You • Twist and Shout • Yellow Submarine • Yesterday • and more.
00295323...$24.99

First 50 Songs
You Should Fingerpick on Guitar
Annie's Song • Blackbird • The Boxer • Classical Gas • Dust in the Wind • Fire and Rain • Greensleeves • Road Trippin' • Shape of My Heart • Tears in Heaven • Time in a Bottle • Vincent (Starry Starry Night) • and more.
00149269 ....$16.99

First 50 Songs You Should
Play on 12-String Guitar
California Dreamin' • Closer to the Heart • Free Fallin' • Give a Little Bit • Hotel California • Leaving on a Jet Plane • Life by the Drop • Over the Hills and Far Away • Solsbury Hill • Space Oddity • Wish You Were Here • You Wear It Well • and more.
00287559...$19.99

First 50 Songs You Should Play on
Acoustic Guitar
Against the Wind • Boulevard of Broken Dreams • Champagne Supernova • Every Rose Has Its Thorn • Fast Car • Free Fallin' • Layla • Let Her Go • Mean • One • Ring of Fire • Signs • Stairway to Heaven • Trouble • Wagon Wheel • Yellow • Yesterday • and more.
00131209 ....$16.99

First 50 Songs
You Should Play on Bass
Blister in the Sun • I Got You (I Feel Good) • Livin' on a Prayer • Low Rider • Money • Monkey Wrench • My Generation • Roxanne • Should I Stay or Should I Go • Uptown Funk • What's Going On • With or Without You • Yellow • and more.
00149189 ....$16.99

First 50 Songs
You Should Play on Solo Guitar
Africa • All of Me • Blue Skies • California Dreamin' • Change the World • Crazy • Dream a Little Dream of Me • Every Breath You Take • Hallelujah • Wonderful Tonight • Yesterday • You Raise Me Up • Your Song • and more.
00288843...$19.99

First 50 Songs
You Should Strum on Guitar
American Pie • Blowin' in the Wind • Daughter • Hey, Soul Sister • Home • I Will Wait • Losing My Religion • Mrs. Robinson • No Woman No Cry • Peaceful Easy Feeling • Rocky Mountain High • Sweet Caroline • Teardrops on My Guitar • Wonderful Tonight • and more.
00148996...$16.99

HAL•LEONARD®
www.halleonard.com

ISBN 978-1-5400-6554-4

Visit Hal Leonard Online at
www.halleonard.com

Contact us:
Hal Leonard
7777 West Bluemound Road
Milwaukee, WI 53213
Email: info@halleonard.com

In Europe, contact:
Hal Leonard Europe Limited
42 Wigmore Street
Marylebone, London, W1U 2RN
Email: info@halleonardeurope.com

In Australia, contact:
Hal Leonard Australia Pty. Ltd.
4 Lentara Court
Cheltenham, Victoria, 3192 Australia
Email: info@halleonard.com.au

CONTENTS

And everything I am
Cries out for You

CORNERSTONE

Words and Music by JONAS MYRIN,
REUBEN MORGAN, ERIC LILJERO
and EDWARD MOTE

FOREVER REIGN

Words and Music by JASON INGRAM
and REUBEN MORGAN

FROM THE INSIDE OUT

Words and Music by
JOEL HOUSTON

LEAD ME TO THE CROSS

Words and Music by
BROOKE LIGERTWOOD

HOSANNA

Words and Music by
BROOKE LIGERTWOOD

I GIVE YOU MY HEART

Words and Music by
REUBEN MORGAN

MIGHTY TO SAVE

Words and Music by BEN FIELDING
and REUBEN MORGAN

With praise

With pedal

THE STAND

Words and Music by
JOEL HOUSTON

OCEANS
(Where Feet May Fail)

Words and Music by JOEL HOUSTON,
MATT CROCKER and SALOMON LIGHTHELM

Moderately slow

STRONGER

Words and Music by BEN FIELDING
and REUBEN MORGAN

WHAT A BEAUTIFUL NAME

Words and Music by BEN FIELDING
and BROOKE LIGERTWOOD

With freedom

Moderately, in tempo

WHO YOU SAY I AM

Words and Music by REUBEN MORGAN
and BEN FIELDING

Slowly, in 2

The Best
PRAISE & WORSHIP
Songbooks for Piano

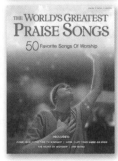

Above All
THE PHILLIP KEVEREN SERIES
15 beautiful praise song piano solo arrangements by Phillip Keveren. Includes: Above All • Agnus Dei • Breathe • Draw Me Close • He Is Exalted • I Stand in Awe • Step by Step • We Fall Down • You Are My King (Amazing Love) • and more.
00311024 Piano Solo..................................$12.99

Blended Worship Piano Collection
Songs include: Amazing Grace (My Chains Are Gone) • Be Thou My Vision • Cornerstone • Fairest Lord Jesus • Great Is Thy Faithfulness • How Great Is Our God • I Will Rise • Joyful, Joyful, We Adore Thee • Lamb of God • Majesty • Open the Eyes of My Heart • Praise to the Lord, the Almighty • Shout to the Lord • 10,000 Reasons (Bless the Lord) • Worthy Is the Lamb • Your Name • and more.
00293528 Piano Solo $17.99

Blessings
THE PHILLIP KEVEREN SERIES
Phillip Keveren delivers another stellar collection of piano solo arrangements perfect for any reverent or worship setting: Blessed Be Your Name • Blessings • Cornerstone • Holy Spirit • This Is Amazing Grace • We Believe • Your Great Name • Your Name • and more.
00156601 Piano Solo $12.99

The Best Praise & Worship Songs Ever
80 all-time favorites: Awesome God • Breathe • Days of Elijah • Here I Am to Worship • I Could Sing of Your Love Forever • Open the Eyes of My Heart • Shout to the Lord • We Bow Down • dozens more.
00311057 P/V/G..............................$22.99

The Big Book of Praise & Worship
Over 50 worship favorites are presented in this popular "Big Book" series collection. Includes: Always • Cornerstone • Forever Reign • I Will Follow • Jesus Paid It All • Lord, I Need You • Mighty to Save • Our God • Stronger • 10,000 Reasons (Bless the Lord) • This Is Amazing Grace • and more.
00140795 P/V/G $24.99

Contemporary Worship Duets
arr. Bill Wolaver
Contains 8 powerful songs carefully arranged by Bill Wolaver as duets for intermediate-level players: Agnus Dei • Be unto Your Name • He Is Exalted • Here I Am to Worship • I Will Rise • The Potter's Hand • Revelation Song • Your Name.
00290593 Piano Duets $10.99

The Best of Passion
Over 40 worship favorites featuring the talents of David Crowder, Matt Redman, Chris Tomlin, and others. Songs include: Always • Awakening • Blessed Be Your Name • Jesus Paid It All • My Heart Is Yours • Our God • 10,000 Reasons (Bless the Lord) • and more.
00101888 P/V/G $19.99

HAL•LEONARD®
www.halleonard.com

P/V/G = Piano/Vocal/Guitar Arrangements

Prices, contents, and availability subject to change without notice.

Praise & Worship Duets
THE PHILLIP KEVEREN SERIES
8 worshipful duets by Phillip Keveren: As the Deer • Awesome God • Give Thanks • Great Is the Lord • Lord, I Lift Your Name on High • Shout to the Lord • There Is a Redeemer • We Fall Down.
00311203 Piano Duet................................$12.99

Shout to the Lord!
THE PHILLIP KEVEREN SERIES
14 favorite praise songs, including: As the Deer • El Shaddai • Give Thanks • Great Is the Lord • How Beautiful • More Precious Than Silver • Oh Lord, You're Beautiful • A Shield About Me • Shine, Jesus, Shine • Shout to the Lord • Thy Word • and more.
00310699 Piano Solo $14.99

Sunday Solos in the Key of C
CLASSIC & CONTEMPORARY WORSHIP SONGS
22 C-major selections, including: Above All • Good Good Father • His Name Is Wonderful • Holy Spirit • Lord, I Need You • Reckless Love • What a Beautiful Name • You Are My All in All • and more.
00301044 Piano Solo $14.99

The Chris Tomlin Collection – 2nd Edition
15 songs from one of the leading artists and composers in Contemporary Christian music, including the favorites: Amazing Grace (My Chains Are Gone) • Holy Is the Lord • How Can I Keep from Singing • How Great Is Our God • Jesus Messiah • Our God • We Fall Down • and more.
00306951 P/V/G $17.99

Top Christian Downloads
21 of Christian music's top hits are presented in this collection of intermediate level piano solo arrangements. Includes: Forever Reign • How Great Is Our God • Mighty to Save • Praise You in This Storm • 10,000 Reasons (Bless the Lord) • Your Grace Is Enough • and more.
00125051 Piano Solo................................$14.99

Top 25 Worship Songs
25 contemporary worship hits includes: Glorious Day (Passion) • Good, Good Father (Chris Tomlin) • Holy Spirit (Francesca Battistelli) • King of My Heart (John Mark & Sarah McMillan) • The Lion and the Lamb (Big Daddy Weave) • Reckless Love (Cory Asbury) • 10,000 Reasons (Matt Redman) • This Is Amazing Grace (Phil Wickham) • What a Beautiful Name (Hillsong Worship) • and more.
00288610 P/V/G $17.99

Top Worship Downloads
20 of today's chart-topping Christian hits, including: Cornerstone • Forever Reign • Great I Am • Here for You • Lord, I Need You • My God • Never Once • One Thing Remains (Your Love Never Fails) • Your Great Name • and more.
00120870 P/V/G $16.99

The World's Greatest Praise Songs
Shawnee Press
This is a unique and useful collection of 50 of the very best praise titles of the last three decades. Includes: Above All • Forever • Here I Am to Worship • I Could Sing of Your Love Forever • Open the Eyes of My Heart • and so many more.
35022891 P/V/G $19.99